Tanest the Meerkat

Jennifer S. Snyder
Illustrated by Deborah Sullivan

This is a work of fiction. The events and characters described herein are imaginary and are not intended to refer to specific places or living persons. The opinions expressed in this manuscript are solely the opinions of the author and do not represent the opinions or thoughts of the publisher. The author has represented and warranted full ownership and/or legal right to publish all the materials in this book.

Tanest The Meerkat
All Rights Reserved.
Copyright © 2015 Jennifer S. Snyder with Illustrations by Deborah Sullivan
v3.0

Cover Photo © 2015 thinkstockphotos.com. All rights reserved - used with permission.

Author photo by Marc Snyder

This book may not be reproduced, transmitted, or stored in whole or in part by any means, including graphic, electronic, or mechanical without the express written consent of the publisher except in the case of brief quotations embodied in critical articles and reviews.

Outskirts Press, Inc.
http://www.outskirtspress.com

ISBN: 978-1-4787-4292-0

Outskirts Press and the "OP" logo are trademarks belonging to Outskirts Press, Inc.

PRINTED IN THE UNITED STATES OF AMERICA

*This book is dedicated to my granddaughter Tanest Arabella Rose.
Memere's Angel.*

It was the night before her birthday as Tanest the meer-Kat was being tucked into bed, her mommy asked "baby Tanest what do you want for your birthday?"

After thinking Tanest said "I want something that I can love forever and ever."

Daddy meerkat said "I think we can do that."

After her parents kissed Tanest good night she quickly fell asleep.

Tanest woke up with the sun the next morning. Sitting beside her on the pillow was a little fairy. "What's your name?" Tanest asked.

"Destiny." the fairy replied. "You need to get up. We have to find your birthday present."

"Oh-boy, something I will love forever." Tanest yelled.

Tanest quickly got dressed and followed the fairy outside.

When they got outside Pockets the squirrel was waiting. "Good morning Pockets." Tanest said.

"And good morning to you birthday girl. I am here to help you find your birthday present."

"But Destiny is helping me." said Tanest.

"Pockets will help you from here. I have to be somewhere else." said Destiny.

"Ok thank you," said Tanest. Pockets told Tanest to follow him.

As they were walking through the forest Pockets said "I have a trick to show you."

All excited Tanest said "I love to learn new things. This is going to be exciting."

They came upon a large stump. "This is what I am going to show you today Tanest." said Pockets. "We can climb up this stump and have a higher view to find Gorf. He is going to take you to the pond and show you what he can do."

Tanest had never climbed a stump before. She watched Pockets and did what he did. Before Tanest knew it she was standing on the stump looking all around her.

A little ways away they spotted Gorf the frog hopping backwards as he always did.

"Good morning Tanest, good morning Pockets." Gorf bellowed out with every hop. "Look at you, Tanest, up on that stump. Looks like Pockets has taught you something today. Happy birthday to you."

"Thank you." Tanest said as she and Pockets climbed down the stump.

"I have to go now. I have someplace else to be. See you later," said Pockets and he scurried off into the forest.

Tanest the Meerkat walled alongside Gorf the frog, hopping backwards when they came to a pond. Tanest looked to the left then the right and said to Gorf "This pond is to big. How are we going to get around it?"

"We are going to go over it," said Gorf. "That is what I am going to teach you today. You just hop from lilly pad to lilly pad until you get to the other side. But you had better jump forward so you can see where you're going. I have lived in this pond my whole life and know where the best path is so follow me Tanest."

As Tanest hopped along she started giggling. Learning to do new things is a lot of fun she thought.

Once they reached the other side Salami the Salamander was waiting. "Good morning Gorf. Good morning Tanest and happy birthday too." Salami said.

"Good morning Salami," they both said.

"Well Tanest it's time for me to hop along. I have someplace else I have to be. But you have some more tricks to learn on your way to find your birthday present. So long." And with that, he hopped away.

Tanest's face lit up. She was having so much fun with her friends she forgot she was looking for her birthday present. Something she would love forever and ever.

"Salami what are you going to teach me today?" asked Tanest.

"Follow me and I will show you." said Salami.

As they walked along the path they came to a huge mud puddle.

"Salami how are we going to get across without getting all muddy?" Tanest asked.

"That is what I am going to teach you Tanest. Do you see that hollow log on top of the mud puddle?" said Salami.

"Yes." Tanest replied.

"We are going to crawl through it to get to the other side without getting muddy. Just follow me and do what I do," explained Salami.

So Tanest followed, even swinging her tail from side to side like Salami did.

When they came out the other side Tanest looked down and had no mud on her.

Sitting on top of a rock was their friend Daphne the Weasel.

"Good morning Daphne." said Salami.

"Good morning Salami. Good morning Tanest. I hear it is your birthday." said Daphne.

"Yes it is. I am looking for my birthday present. My friends have been helping me." said Tanest. "I have had a lot of fun this morning."

"Daphne will take you from here Tanest. I have somewhere else I have to be." and he scurried off.

"What did you ask for Tanest?" Daphne asked.

Tanest replied "I asked for something I could love forever and ever."

"Wow that sounds like a great gift." said Daphne. "I can help you find it. I am a great hunter. Just follow me."

So Tanest followed Daphne through the forest.

Daphne said "When I am looking for food I put my nose to the ground until I smell something good then follow that smell until I find it."

"But I don't know what I am smelling for." said Tanest.

"You'll know it when you pick up the right scent," said Daphne.

So off they went side by side down the path. After a few minutes, Tanest found a scent. It smelled like a birthday cake. Daphne smelled it too. They followed the smell a little longer until Tanest realized she was in a clearing.

She looked up to see her whole family and all her friends who then yelled "Surprise!!"

Tanest was so surprised she jumped and let out a great big laugh.

She saw her mom, dad, all her grandparents, aunts, uncles, and all her friends including the ones who helped her all morning.

She was so happy. They all threw her a big surprise party just for her with the biggest prettiest cake she ever saw.

Tanest ran to her mom and dad and hugged them both.

"Thank you." she said. "I got just what I wanted. Something I will love forever and ever. My whole family and all my friends."

With a kiss to Tanest's forehead her mother said, "And a gift that will love you forever and ever. Happy Birthday Tanest. We all love you."